ART
KEEP OUT
NO
RAISE
MOST WEDNESDAYS.
after.
Je ne sais pas.
artifice
...BUT I LOVE YOU.
F=ma
WISE UP!
this.

25¢
DIEGO
32¢
Vapour
87
boots
ALBERT.
carpe diem!
SEE YOU AT BINGO!
Automatic Teller
GREEN...
requiem
陳志勇
B.
TROUBLE TROUBLE
TROUBLE TROUBLE
TROUBLE TROUBLE